101
Nature Activities
for Kids

Jane Sanborn and Elizabeth Rundle

HEALTHY
LEARNING™

ISBN: 978-1-60679-156-1
Library of Congress Control Number: 2011920905
Cover design: Brenden Murphy
Book layout: Studio J Art & Design
Front cover photos: Will Ostendorff (center), iStockphoto/Thinkstock (left),
    Sanborn Western Camps (right)
Text photos: Jane Sanborn, Elizabeth Rundle, and Sanborn Western Camps
    staff members (unless otherwise noted)

Healthy Learning
P.O. Box 1828
Monterey, CA 93942
www.healthylearning.com

Dedication

To Jamie, Raina, Jack, Julia, and Rebecca

Acknowledgments

Thank you to the thousands of campers and staff members at Sanborn Western Camps and High Trails Outdoor Education Center who have developed, shared, and refined most of the activities in this book over the past 60 years. Their joy in exploring the out-of-doors continues to be our source of inspiration.

We also wish to acknowledge the contributions of our many friends and colleagues in the American Camp Association. We're confident that the ideas for any number of the activities included came from you—during conferences, educational sessions, or just informal conversations. Providing opportunities for children to create a personal connection with the natural world has long been a mission of the camping community. We hope this book will provide a few activities you didn't already know about or remind you of some you may have forgotten about.

Although several of the staff members at Sanborn Western Camps have helped in the creation of this book, we are especially grateful for the work of Ariella Rogge who sorted through tens of thousands of photos to help us locate the ones we knew we took but couldn't find when we needed them. And thank you to Andrew Jones, who read the entire manuscript and kept us from making many faux pas related to plural nouns and singular verbs. He also cleaned up our punctuation in really important ways.

Finally, we have really enjoyed working with Angie Perry of Coaches Choice/Healthy Learning. She graciously gave us a deadline extension when we noted that September 1 was not a practical timetable for summer camp directors. She has also answered every question in an extremely timely way and provided us with help and suggestions whenever we asked.

Contents

#1: Magic Eye
#2: Do You See?
#3: Blindfold Hike
#4: Blindfolded Partners
#5: Camera
#6: Paint Chip Hike
#7: Meet a Tree
#8: Soundscape
#9: Deer Stalker
#10: Asteroid Belt
#11: Sense of Smell Hike
#12: Team Sense
#13: Martian Hike
#14: Bag of Rocks
#15: Nature Sounds
#16: Flubber

#17: I Spy Way Up High
#18: Cloud Races
#19: 100-Inch Hike
#20: Naming Game
#21: The Question Game
#22: Silent Hike
#23: Special Spots
#24: Nature Writing
#25: Journal Writing
#26: Poetry Writing—Haiku
#27: Poetry Writing—Vertical Poetry
#28: Poetry Writing—Cinquain
#29: Past and Future

Introduction

We have long known that magical things happen when children spend time in the natural world. Now, thanks to Richard Louv and the Children & Nature Network, the research is available to support our intuitive understanding that nature is not only good for young people, but also essential to their healthy development.

Time spent in nature reduces ADHD and childhood depression; it inspires children to be more creative and more resilient; it calms them and, at the same time, excites all of their senses. As Louv says, children who spend time in nature are "happier, healthier, and smarter."

This information is reassuring to those of us who work in outdoor youth development. It also places more responsibility upon us. Now, understanding the importance of what we do, we must take every opportunity to not only get young people out-of-doors, but also to create opportunities for them to feel a personal connection with the natural world. We must be more intentional in our purpose and in our work.

The good news is that it does not take a college degree in natural sciences to inspire children in the outdoors. The most important qualities for an adult sharing the outdoors with children are enthusiasm, interest, and an active sense of wonder. As Rachel Carson said, "If a child is to keep alive his inborn sense of wonder...he needs the companionship of at least one adult who can share it, rediscovering with him the joy, excitement, and mystery of the world we live in."

The activities in this book have all been used and tested at Sanborn Western Camps and High Trails Outdoor Education Center in central Colorado. They are designed to be used in any outdoor location from Maine to California, and most of them are appropriate for a backyard or city park as well as for the forest, a meadow, or the beach.

In general, we have chosen activities that do not need a lot of equipment or much preparation time. Many of these activities are designed to enhance the use of our five senses and, perhaps, most importantly, our sense of wonder.

Sensory Awareness Activities

The first step in increasing a child's *understanding* of the natural world is to increase his *awareness* of it. When the five senses are fully awakened, learning and enjoyment come rapidly. Stretching the use of children's senses heightens their sense of wonder, their appreciation of beauty, and their imagination. It makes them more receptive to their world, to their cohabitants on planet Earth, and to themselves.

The activities in this section can be used as an introduction to the out-of-doors for novices, or as a reminder of its wonders for veterans. Most of the activities can be done in a schoolyard or city park, as well as in a forest or a meadow. Because this chapter deals with sensory perception, all five senses are included in activity descriptions. Guides must be aware of any harmful or poisonous plants in the area that should not be tasted or touched.

"Every child should have mud pies, grasshoppers,
water-bugs, tadpoles, frogs, mud turtles, elderberries,
wild strawberries, acorns, chestnuts, trees to climb,
brooks to wade in, waterlilies, woodchucks, bats, bees,
butterflies, various animals to pet, hayfields, pinecones,
rocks to roll, sand, snakes, huckleberries and hornets;
and any child who has been deprived of these
has been deprived of the best part of his education."
—Luther Burbank

Activity #1: Magic Eye

This activity stresses the full use of the sense of sight. Subtle patterns, textures, forms, and colors pop into clear focus through the "magic eye." A magic eye can be a mat for framing, a knothole in a piece of wood, or even a circle made with the thumb and index finger. The magic eye can be held at varying distances from the eye to focus on different things. Start by asking each camper to hold the magic eye next to his eye and to look through the hole at any object he chooses. He can then slowly stretch his arm out toward the object, always looking through the magic eye. When his arm is at full length, he should look carefully at what he has framed. He may want to walk up and examine it closely. Each child should then choose another object for scrutiny through the magic eye.

Activity #2: Do You See?

This exercise is valuable in helping campers to become aware of the common habit of looking without seeing. Without explaining why, ask group members to look in one direction for 60 seconds. Then, have them close their eyes and ask them questions about the area they just viewed. Were there clouds in the sky? Did they notice any animal signs? How many colors did they see? What was the largest thing they saw? What was the smallest? Participants may then open their eyes and take another look at the area. Ask them what they see this time that they didn't notice the first time. Repeat the exercise and you will find that the campers have become much more observant.

Hemera/Thinkstock

Activity #3: Blindfold Hike

Most people depend too much on sight for evaluation of the world around them and thus miss out on other perceptions they might enjoy. Removing the use of sight for a short time helps remind everyone of the wonderful sounds, textures, smells, and tastes which are too frequently ignored.

In this activity, six or seven participants line up behind one person who acts as the leader of the group. Everyone except the leader puts a blindfold on and the leader takes the group on a short walk, helping his followers to sense their environment more fully.

Ask the campers to relax and concentrate first on their sense of hearing by listening to the sound of walking. Can they tell what they are walking on (e.g., grass, asphalt, gravel)? What noises do they hear? They can first try to identify the source of each sound and then imagine trying to write the noises they hear. Now, ask them to turn off the labeling part of their brain and "feel" the sounds with no thought of how they originate. They can imagine that they are in the middle of a symphony orchestra.

Next, walk into a shaded area. Can they feel the difference between the sunny area and the shaded area? Can they feel a change in temperature? Each guide can help his blindfolded followers to touch rocks, trees, soil, and anything else within their immediate environment.

Now, ask the participants to concentrate on their sense of smell. Ask them to smell bark, grass, pine needles, soil, the air. Can they identify pleasant aromas? Are any of the odors familiar? Do the smells remind them of anything?

Finally, campers can concentrate on their sense of taste. Guides can give each camper a pine needle or a blade of grass to roll around with his tongue to determine its shape and texture. Is the taste stronger than they expected when they bite into it? Try a needle from another kind of tree or a blade from a different type of grass. Is the taste different? Could they differentiate between these two trees or types of grass by taste alone?

Activity #4: Blindfolded Partners

In addition to accenting other senses by removing the sense of sight, this game helps to create feelings of trust and responsibility for a partner. Each player is also placed in the unique position of being a guide for a blindfolded partner, which heightens sensitivity and awareness for the natural surroundings. The group is divided into pairs, and one member of each partnership is blindfolded. The other partner helps the "blind" person walk around, giving him things to touch, smell, and taste. The guide needs to be especially aware of the safety of his blindfolded partner, and he should do everything he can to help him sense the environment fully. After about five minutes, the partners can change roles.

Activity #5: Camera

Players are divided into pairs and within each pair, one partner is the photographer while the other person is the "camera." The photographer's job is to find a beautiful or interesting view and point his partner (the camera) toward this view. Like all cameras, the shutter of the camera (the participant's eyes) are closed until the photographer snaps the picture. Once the photographer has his camera pointed at the "picture," he opens the shutter by squeezing his partner's elbow. Encourage the photographer to be creative and take pictures from different angles. After a number of pictures have been taken, the partners should exchange roles. Once both partners have been the camera, give the participants a sheet of paper and colored pencils and ask them to draw their favorite "photo." Do not allow them to go back and look—they must draw from memory. Once they have completed their drawings with as much detail as they can remember, have them go back and compare their drawings to the actual pictures.

Hemera/Thinkstock

Activity #6: Paint Chip Hike

Looking closely at colors in the natural world provides an always surprising and sometimes amazing awareness of the variety and richness to be found outdoors. Go to a hardware store and stock up on paint chips in various colors—pinks, blues, greens, reds, yellows—that do not seem like they would be in a natural setting. Before the hike, hand each child one or more paint chips and have them try to find as many things in nature as possible that match their color. It might be a purple flower or a neon yellow lichen.

Next, ask each child to hide or camouflage his paint chip somewhere in the natural environment. Once all the chips are hidden, send the group out to find the paint chips. The winner is either the camper who finds the most colors or the person who hid his chip so well that no one could find it.

Activity #7: Meet a Tree

Lead a small group of blindfolded participants on a short walk, allowing them to concentrate on their less used senses by taking away the most highly used sense—sight. Guide the blindfolded players through a variety of sensory experiences—sunlight, shade, open areas, trees, grass, rocks—always going slowly and building their confidence in you as their leader. Now, leave each blindfolded camper at a different tree. Tell each one to learn as much as possible about his tree by feeling, smelling, listening, and even tasting. After a few minutes, bring the participants away from their trees, remove the blindfolds, and ask each one to find his tree. If they have trouble finding their tree, discuss how successful players identified their trees and then repeat the exercise. During the debriefing time for this activity, participants can share how they felt about "their" trees. This activity can also lead to a great discussion about the needs of individuals compared with the needs of a community.

Activity #8: Soundscape

Give each member of your group a piece of blank paper and some colored pencils and have each one spread out in a natural setting. If possible, place members of the group in two different environments (e.g., half of the group in a forest and the other half in a meadow). Ask everyone to sit quietly and listen for birds chirping, leaves blowing, and other sounds in nature for 10 minutes. As they listen to each distinct sound, ask them to think about what that sound "looks" like. What color is it? Is it smooth, wavy, or rough? Is it loud or soft? Once they have an idea what the sound looks like, they can use their colored pencils to draw a diagram of each of the different sounds they hear. Ask group members to share their diagrams with each other and then choose a new location and create another sound tapestry. Following is an example of a small sound tapestry in a summer meadow.

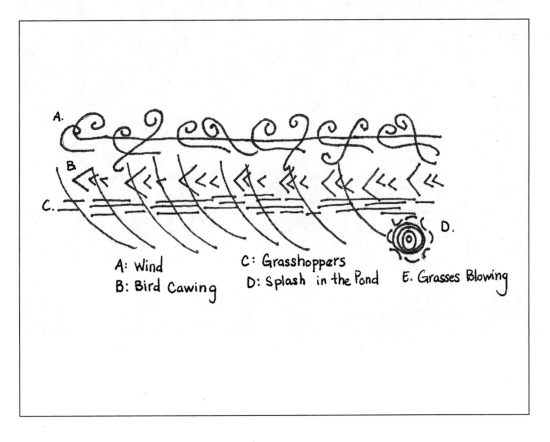

A: Wind
B: Bird Cawing
C: Grasshoppers
D: Splash in the Pond
E. Grasses Blowing

Activity #9: Deer Stalker

Two players are blindfolded and one is designated as the deer and the other as the stalker. The other players in the group form a large circle around these two in order to provide a protected area for the blindfolded players. Members of the circle may gently redirect the deer and stalker to keep them within this area. Within the confines of this circle, the stalker tries to tag the deer by listening for footsteps, heavy breaths, and other deer noises, while the deer tries to keep away from the stalker. The outside circle must be absolutely quiet, for any noise will be distracting to the blindfolded participants. If the stalker does not catch the deer within a certain time limit, the deer wins the round and two new participants are chosen.

Activity #10: Asteroid Belt

In this space-age scenario, a spaceship tries to maneuver its way safely through a crowded field of asteroids. One blindfolded player represents the spaceship. The remaining players become the asteroids and take up random positions in an area approximately 30 feet long and 10 feet wide. The spaceship then tries to move through the full length of the asteroid belt without bumping into any of them. Fortunately, the spaceship is equipped with radar so that when it approaches one of the asteroids, the asteroid must emit a "beep, beep" sound in warning. If the spaceship successfully completes the trip, another player is selected to pilot the craft and the game continues. If the ship crashes into an asteroid, the destroying asteroid becomes the new pilot and returns to the starting point to begin a new game.

Activity #11: Sense of Smell Hike

Take a hike and ask campers to focus on their sense of smell to explore the natural world around them. Which flowers and grasses have odors? Why do they have these scents? Have them smell the bark of different trees. Is there a scent that makes them think of something else? Have them smell the soil in different areas. Can they learn anything about the soil from its scent? What does the air smell like? What can they learn about the natural world by focusing on their sense of smell?

iStockphoto/Thinkstock

Activity #12: Team Sense

Four people act together as a team, and each member has only one sense (i.e., one person can smell, one person can taste, one person can hear, and one person can feel). Another participant acts as the leader. The sensory participants are blindfolded and the leader gives the team an object from nature, which each player experiences and then describes to the rest of the team from his sensory perspective. The point of the game is to put all the team's information together in order to identify the object. This can be a game for one team or a race between two or more teams.

Activity #13: Martian Hike

Taking a new perspective increases sensory awareness by reopening eyes and ears to those things which have become so common that campers no longer fully appreciate them. By taking the role of visitors from another planet, your group can explore the Earth for the first time, renewing not only their understanding but also their sense of wonder.

The secret of a Martian Hike is to use all the senses as if everything were totally new and different. Ask the participants questions like: Do trees exist on Mars? Are Martian trees green? Why are there trees on Earth? Why are they green? This type of questioning can be used for anything you find along the hike.

Remind the participants that, as Martians, they might be tiny. How does the grass look? Gravel? Trees? What animals might frighten you? Or, as Martians, they might be giants. How does the earth seem from this perspective? Throughout your explorations, encourage the Martians to share their discoveries with one another and to try to develop plausible reasons for the existence of the things they find.

iStockphoto/Thinkstock

Activity #14: Bag of Rocks

Have everyone find or choose a rock from a pile. Ask each person to get to know his rock. How does it feel? How many sides does it have? What color is it? Does it have any marks on it? Is it heavy or light? Have everyone put their rocks in a bag and mix them up. Each person then reaches into the bag to find his rock. If participants cannot identify their rocks by touch alone, take the rocks out of the bag, which should make it easier. How easy is it to find a particular rock? How is one rock different from another rock? This activity can be done with pinecones, blades of grass, shells, or any other abundant natural object.

Activity #15: Nature Sounds

Ask campers to spread out and be seated in a natural area. The group is then given five minutes to see which participant can make the longest list of things they hear in the natural world during that time. Compare lists and try again. The longer they listen, the more they will hear.

iStockphoto/Thinkstock

Activity #16: Flubber

This activity is a good, quick way to lead into other sensory awareness activities. To make "flubber," give campers the following instructions:

- Mix two 16-ounce boxes of cornstarch and about two cups of water in a bowl, then add another 1 3/8 cups of water.
- Mix by hand to ensure an even consistency. Do not push through the mixture as if mixing batter, but rather keep lifting from the bottom of the bowl to the top until an even consistency is reached.
- The flubber should flow when you tip the bowl, but feel like a solid when you hit it or rub your finger across the surface. If it is too thick to flow, just add a little water. If it is slightly soupy, add a little more cornstarch.

Blindfold the campers and have them first use their sense of touch. Is the flubber a liquid or a solid or both? How can they make it become a solid or liquid? Ask them to punch the flubber in the bowl hard and quick, then gently and slowly. When does it seem to be a liquid? When does it seem to be a solid? After you have taken off the blindfolds, let the campers play with the flubber using their other senses and see if they can make other discoveries. Flubber is messy—use it outside!

2

Sense of Wonder and Perspective

The sense of wonder is that natural sense of curiosity children have, and yet it takes constant cultivation in order for it to continue to grow and remain with them into adulthood. Wonder can be encouraged by slowing down, asking questions, and taking time to see the big picture along with the small details that make up the natural world around us.

Research has shown that children who feel a personal connection with the natural world are happier, healthier, and more likely to care deeply about the environment as adults. The activities in this section encourage this personal connection by inspiring a sense of wonder and broadened perspectives through observation, exploration, and discovery. Some of the activities are specifically targeted to teach something about personal responsibility in caring for the planet, as well as present steps that individuals can take to help conserve and preserve the natural world.

> *"The Aspens whisper to me. The aroma of Earth is all*
> *around me. For only about the third time in my life,*
> *I am truly calm. I feel as if I can see all, yet as if I only*
> *see a little, as if my eyes are only half open...I feel free."*
> —Sixth grade student

Activity #17: I Spy Way Up High

Find a comfortable place for campers to lie down and relax. Ask the group to search for shapes in the clouds and let their imaginations go to work. This activity is a simple way to allow campers just to be still.

Activity #18: Cloud Races

Have campers lie down, look up in the sky, and pick a cloud to watch race by. Choose a point as a finish line and see whose cloud crosses it first.

Hemera/Thinkstock

Activity #19: 100-Inch Hike

Shrinking the field of perception often adds to awareness. By closely examining a very small area, wonders can be discovered which might otherwise be overlooked. In the 100-Inch Hike, campers are each given a piece of string 100 inches long. Each camper places it on the ground and carefully explores the area that stretches the string. Things to look for include: signs of animals, birds, or insects; distinctive characteristics of any plant along the trail; textures of soil or sand; different colors, etc. Campers may wish to record their findings and share them with other members of the group. A variation on this activity is to shape a wire clothes hanger into a square and examine the area inside the square.

Activity #20: Naming Game

Trappers and early explorers often conducted the earliest surveys of the West and were responsible for naming and mapping many things. While campers are walking along, have them observe geographic features, plants, insects, birds, trees, etc., as if they have never seen those objects before. Have them give the items they find names based on physical characteristics, similarity to other plants which exist in other places, the name of the discoverer, etc. Following is a sample *Official New Plant Discovery Form* to fill out for any plants they name. "Official discovery forms" can be created for each specific topic that is in the lesson being taught.

iStockphoto/Thinkstock

Official New Plant Discovery Form

Plant height _____ Leaf length_____ Leaf width_____

Draw a picture of the plant leaf. Be sure to show the shape, size, stem edges, and any other details.

Draw a picture of the plant seed.

Is the plant's stem woody? What kind of soil is the plant growing in? (Moist? Dry? Gravelly? Sandy? Clay?)

How many flowers or seed pods does the plant have? What kind are they? Where are they located?

How do you think the plant spreads its seeds?

What could animals use this plant for?

What could humans use this plant for?

Activity #21: The Question Game

Cultivating the sense of wonder naturally sparks questions, and it is important to emphasize that questions are encouraged. This activity allows for campers to let questions flow through their minds. Have them find a place to sit comfortably and look around. Each child should have a pencil and a piece of paper to write his questions on as he thinks of them. It may take a little guidance and prompting to start the thought process and then to keep it going in the right direction. After a period of time, allow some time for sharing. Following are some sample questions:

- In what ways can you use pine needles (or leaves, sticks, rocks, flowers)?
- Why do horses sleep standing up?
- Where do rainbows come from?
- What purposes do rocks have?
- Why do certain trees grow on one side of a hill and not the other?
- What if trees did not exist?

Activity #22: Silent Hike

Explain to the participants that they are going to take a silent hike and that they will be looking for cards that have been placed along the trail. The cards will provide an action for the campers to perform or a question for them to consider. Remind them that this part of the activity should be conducted silently. The leader, who has written the cards ahead of time, goes first and places the cards strategically along the trail; the campers follow, leaving about 30 to 45 seconds in between each person so that everyone can take their time. The last person, preferably a counselor, should pick up the cards as he walks along the trail.

Cards might include the following questions or commands:

- Look around…what colors do you see?
- Feel the ground.
- Silently tell this tree a secret.
- Slow down.
- Look up.
- What if you had wings?
- Dance a jig!
- What if the oceans dried up?
- Smell this flower.
- Place your hand on a tree that you like.
- Breathe slowly and deeply—the air you breathed in was breathed out by this tree, and the air you breathed out was breathed in by this tree!
- Listen…what do you hear?
- Would you rather take a walk in the sunshine or the moonlight?
- If you were a hawk, how would you see things differently?
- What do you appreciate about nature?
- What can you do to help nature?
- What dreams do you have?
- Find a plant that draws your attention.
- How do clouds make you feel?
- Lie under this tree and look up at the branches.
- If you were an animal, where would you build your home? Why?
- What kind of weather do you like best?
- What is your favorite season?
- Remember a time when you saw something in nature you've never seen before… how did that make you feel?
- How many different shades of green do you see?

- What memories of nature do you have?
- Imagine you are a tree…how do you feel when it rains?

When everyone has completed the silent hike, gather the group and ask them to share any thoughts or discoveries they had during the walk.

Activity #23: Special Spots

When out on a hike, look for an area where campers can spread out and each one can find a special spot. Explain to the campers that they will be like giants in their special spots, so they will need to inspect them closely to discover what is going on in them. When they enter the special spots, they will be entering little communities that already existed before they arrived, so it is important not to do anything that would disturb or damage the spots. Have them look carefully at rocks and sticks. Ask them: What shapes are the rocks and sticks? Where do you think they came from? What living things do you find? How do those living things depend on the nonliving things in your spot? What sounds or smells do you experience? Encourage them just to sit quietly and look at the view. This activity is also a great time to complete the writing exercises from Activity #24 through Activity #28.

Activity #24: Nature Writing

Writing even a few lines about the natural world can deepen the writer's personal connection with nature. This activity can be used with Activity #23: Special Spots. After participants have spent time exploring their special spots, give them each a pencil and paper and ask them to write one line or more about something they have observed. For young people who have difficulty writing, help them narrow the focus of their observation—it is often easier to write something about one branch of a tree than it is to write about a forest.

iStockphoto/Thinkstock

Activity #25: Journal Writing

For multiday programs, keeping a nature journal is a great way to help participants expand their observational powers. Set aside a time each day and lead participants to a quiet place where they can write their observations and thoughts. The journal writings can be private or shared, depending on the preferences of the group.

Activity #26: Poetry Writing—Haiku

The natural world inspires poetry, and it is fun to let the group create their own poems while outdoors. Haiku is a specific form of nature-based poetry, which can be helpful in inspiring beginning poets. Haiku includes three lines and a total of 17 or fewer syllables and often includes a season word. The following haikus are by seventeenth century Japanese poet Matsuo Basho:

No one travels
Along this way but I,
This autumn evening.

Clouds appear
And bring to men a chance to rest
From looking at the moon.

When everyone has had a chance to compose a haiku, give those who wish to share the opportunity to read them to the group.

Activity #27: Poetry Writing—Vertical Poetry

Vertical poetry is another form of writing that can help campers express themselves by providing a framework for their poems. Ask each member of your group to choose a word that captures the feeling of the location you are in. They can then use each letter of the word to begin a line of their poem. Following is an example of a vertical poem using the word *trees*:

Towering over me

Roots deeply grounded in the richness of the soil, supporting, strengthening

Emerald green leaves, twisting, turning, blowing, whispering

Enriching with the wisdom of nature

Summer days spent lying below your branches, in your shade—peaceful and protected.

Activity #28: Poetry Writing—Cinquain

Using the cinquain form makes it possible for everyone to be successful as a nature poet.

A cinquain has five lines. The first line is a one-word noun. For example:

    (a) Tree   (b) Meadow   (c) Hawk

The second line is a two-word description of the first line. Examples:

    (a) Green, leafy   (b) Open, endless   (c) Patient, watching

The third line is three words telling of some action. Examples:

    (a) Shading the earth   (b) Gold leaves blowing   (c) Soaring through sky

The fourth line is four words and expresses an emotion or asks a question. Examples:

    (a) I have come home   (b) I want to run   (c) Where do you live?

The fifth line is another single word similar to the first line. Examples:

    (a) Sentinel   (b) Grass   (c) Redtail

Poem Examples:

(a)	(b)	(c)
Tree	Meadow	Hawk
Green, leafy	Open, endless	Patient, watching
Shading the earth	Gold leaves blowing	Soaring through sky
I have come home	I want to run	Where do you live?
Sentinel	Grass	Redtail

After each instruction, give everyone time to complete that step before going on to the next line. When everyone has finished, ask anyone who would like to share his poem with the group to read his aloud.

Activity #29: Past and Future

This activity can be done anywhere outside. Ask the campers to imagine what the location they are in was like 100 years ago and discuss their thoughts. What things can they see now that would not have been there 100 years ago? What things might they have seen 100 years ago that they cannot see now? What things are the same? Divide the group into smaller ones and ask each group to make a sketch of what they think the place might look like 100 years from now.

iStockphoto/Thinkstock

Activity #30: Universal Journey

Find a place outside with a good view and ask the members of your group to think about perspective. Ask them what they think perspective means. Have them lie flat on their stomachs and look at the world from the point of view of an ant. How would a tree look from this perspective? How would a blade of grass look? Now, ask them to stand up and pretend to be a hawk, looking down. How would a tree or the grass look to a soaring bird?

The following journey of the imagination can be used to help broaden perspective. Ask the participants to make themselves comfortable and close their eyes. Tell them you are going to take them on a Universal Journey. The leader reads the following script, filling in the appropriate place names:

> Let's consider where we are right now from several different perspectives. Imagine that you are able to leave your body and look at this whole group from the outside. First, we are going to expand our perspectives.
>
> Right now we are sitting on a hill at _____. We are floating above, looking down at ourselves. Now, we are floating high enough so we can see the whole state. Do we look bigger or smaller from this perspective?
>
> Now, let's float even higher so we can see the whole United States—Texas, Florida, California. I can see trucks carrying oranges from Florida and trains carrying steel from Pittsburgh. I see coal trains and railcars filled with wheat moving east and manufactured goods moving west. The whole country is tied together by highways, railroad tracks, airplanes. How do we look from this perspective?
>
> As we float even higher, we can see the whole Earth. Wow, is it beautiful! Can you see Africa and India? China and France? What do you think the young people in these countries are doing right now? What are they thinking about? When we look at them from this perspective, they seem closer to us.
>
> Now, we are going even farther. First, we see our whole solar system—the sun and its planets. As we continue to move away, the Earth and even the sun grow smaller and smaller. If the Earth were the size of a pebble one inch in circumference, the sun would be about 100 yards away. On this same scale, the nearest star would be 341 miles away. If we could travel at the speed of light (approximately 186,000 miles per second), it would take us over four years to get to the nearest star. Traveling at this speed, a billion years could pass on Earth in what seems like an instant to us.
>
> But in our imaginations, we are going to travel much faster, through the 100 million stars of the Milky Way galaxy—until we can see the whole galaxy. It looks like a giant pinwheel of light. A dense cluster of stars in

the center is circled by spiraling arms of stars. We know our sun is on one of these arms. Perhaps we could see it if we had telescopic eyes.

But our trip isn't over yet. We are going to zoom away from the Milky Way galaxy, through perhaps 100 billion other galaxies, each containing hundreds of millions or hundreds of billions of stars, to the edge of the Universe. Look toward Earth now. What do you see? We have reached the broadest perspective we know about. From this point of view, even our galaxy would seem like a tiny speck in the strongest telescope.

Now, we're ready for the return trip. Close your eyes so the tremendous speed won't make you dizzy. Through the Universe and billions of whirling galaxies and back to the Milky Way galaxy and then to our own solar system. Look, there is the Earth. How do you feel about the Earth now? Does it seem bigger or smaller than it did before?

Continuing to zoom in, we see the United States, then our state, then _____. Let's bring our imaginations back to our bodies and look at the things around us from this perspective. Do they look any different to you now?

Ablestock.com

Activity #31: Tree Talk

The more people appreciate and understand something, the less likely they are to harm it. This concept is especially true in the natural world, and Tree Talk helps emphasize an attitude that can help young people and adults make intelligent decisions in regard to our environment. Have your group encircle a tree and say a few words about the tree, then ask each participant to speak about the tree for 15 seconds. These comments can be descriptive or imaginative. Participants might consider the tree's height, age, coloring, special markings, leaf or needle structure, root systems, conformation of its branches, relationship with birds and animals, what it has "seen" during its lifetime, how it "feels" about losing its leaves, how it likes its location, how it gets along with its neighbors, etc. What other living things are dependent on the tree? What is the tree dependent on? After each person has had an opportunity to speak and everyone feels he really "knows" the tree, the group leader can ask the group if they would like to cut the tree down. Participants are usually opposed to cutting the tree down, and this can lead into a good discussion of appreciation of the natural world. This activity can also be done with any plant or animal as the central focus.

Activity #32: Litter Tree

Create a Litter Tree by untwisting several wire coat hangers, creating long wires with a hook at the end. Next, twist the ends of the hangers together near the hook and "plant" the hook ends in floral wax or stiff clay. Your "tree" will have a twisted wire trunk with many branches spreading out.

Place the tree in a central location and explain to campers that they can bring any pieces of trash they find on the ground and tape them to the Litter Tree. It won't be long before the tree begins to sprout colorful leaves of candy wrappers, soda cans, and any other litter found by the campers. The Litter Tree is a great way to build enthusiasm among campers for picking up litter.

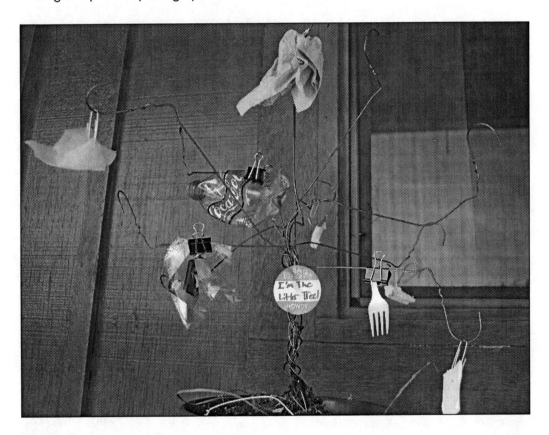

Activity #33: Litter Over Time

Similar to Activity #32: Litter Tree, this activity will help demonstrate how important it is to dispose properly of trash and to pick up any litter the campers may find by illustrating how long it takes specific items to decompose (i.e., break down organic matter from a complex to simple form, mainly through the action of fungi, bacteria or solar radiation). It also demonstrates how important it is to recycle when possible and to dispose of trash properly. Show the group a collection of various objects (or read aloud a list of objects). Ask them to guess the amount of time it takes for each item to decompose.

Following are some items and their average decomposition times. Decomposition times will vary depending on weather and site conditions.

Item	Average Decomposition Time
Piece of paper	2 to 4 weeks
Orange or banana peel	3 to 5 weeks
Candy wrapper	1 to 3 months
Newspaper	3 to 6 months
Carry-out food bag	4 to 8 months
Cigarette butt	2 to 5 years
Cardboard	5 to 7 years
Plastic bag	10 to 20 years
Nylon fabric	30 to 40 years
Plastic six-pack holder	450 years
Aluminum can	200 to 500 years
Styrofoam container	Never
Glass bottle	Never

Are the campers surprised by how long it takes things to decompose? Were the guesses way off? Which of the items listed can be recycled? What is the best way to dispose of each of the items listed? Have the campers seen any of these items outside, perhaps where people have littered? Many people think it is acceptable to leave food items like apple cores or fruit skins on the ground because they are "natural." However, even food takes a long time to break down and can be harmful to any wildlife that might eat it.

iStockphoto/Thinkstock

Activity #34: *The Lorax*

Read this classic fable by Dr. Seuss aloud to your campers and then ask them to share their thoughts. What mistakes did the Once-ler make? What were his motivations? Was the Lorax right every time? What might the Once-ler have done differently? Do humans need to use products from the natural world to live? Are there ways for humans to use natural products without destroying the environment?

3

Activities That Teach
Natural Concepts

The activities in this chapter teach some basic science concepts related to the natural world in a fun, experiential way. Some of the activities help campers understand about the many interconnections of life on Earth—food chains, balances within the natural world, needs for shelter and procreation. Other activities provide interesting ways of teaching and learning specific names and information about local flora and fauna. Still other activities focus on earth science and create exciting learning situations that help campers to become more aware of rocks and soil and the important role the geology of the planet plays in creating an environment that supports life forms.

"I have grown taller from walking with the trees."
—Cedric Wright

Activity #35: Web of Life

You will need a ball of yarn for this activity, which demonstrates the interconnections of all life on Earth. Have everyone form a circle. Stand in the center of the circle, holding the ball of yarn. Ask each of the campers to choose an animal, plant, or other facet of nature that he would like to represent. Holding on to the end of the yarn, give the ball of yarn to the first camper who shares what part of nature he has chosen to represent. Then, as other animals and plants are mentioned, ask the campers if any connections exist between them. If camper A is a "squirrel" and camper B is a "tree," then the squirrel may make a home in the tree and eat the seeds of the tree. Illustrate these connections by passing the yarn from one camper to another whenever a connection is made. Many things will be connected many times—if one camper is representing the Sun, for example, he will have to be connected to everything. Keep the discussion, and the web, going at a quick pace. Then, ask them if it really matters if one item is removed from the web. Is an ant really that important? Have the camper who is the ant gently tug the yarn and see how many others feel it. Did the tree feel it? How about the squirrel? At the end of the discussion, disconnect the web, and have a conversation about what conditions would cause different animals, plants, or other natural objects to disappear (e.g., pollution, development, logging, etc.) Ask them: What has everyone learned about the interconnections on Earth?

Activity #36: Interconnection Lap Sit

Give each player a card printed with the name of an animal or plant that is part of the ecosystem in your area. When everyone is ready, have each player find and join hands with an animal or plant on which he depends for survival. Keep identifying these connections until everyone is joined in a circle. Now, ask the group to perform a lap sit where each person puts his hands on the hips of the person standing in front of him, and then everyone in the group lowers himself so that he is sitting on the lap of the person behind him in a self-supporting circle. All members of an ecosystem are important. If your players don't believe this fact, have one person representing an animal in the middle of the chain stand up.

Activity #37: Food Chain Pyramid

Not only does this active demonstration emphasize the balance necessary in an ecosystem, but it also depicts vividly the collapse of an ecosystem in which one or more members are removed.

To begin, four members of the group are selected to form the base of the pyramid. They are "plants" and each person can choose a specific plant to represent. Three "herbivores" are then chosen to form a second row on top of the kneeling plants. Two "primary carnivores" then ascend the "herbivores." The pyramid is topped off by one secondary carnivore. *Note*: When choosing group members for each pyramid level, try to put larger members on the lower levels and the smallest member on top.

The pyramid might look like the following:

Hawk

Snake   Raccoon

Mouse   Gopher   Small Fish

Dandelion   Parsley   Grass   Algae

When the pyramid is formed, the leader can pull one of the "plants" from the base. The food-chain jumble that ensues is a startling reminder of what can happen in an unbalanced ecosystem.

Variation: To demonstrate the value of diversity within an ecosystem, this activity can be followed by building a broader base with six or seven plants, four or five herbivores, and so on. Usually, the removal of one plant from this pyramid will result in only a partial crash.

Thinkstock Images

Activity #38: Camouflage Hide-and-Seek

One of the most common adaptations in nature is camouflage—the ability of an animal to blend into its environment. This game helps to underscore its importance. It is best to play this game in a forest or an area where there is an abundance of natural cover. Begin by selecting one person to represent the predator. The predator is blindfolded and stands in the center of the play area. The remaining players represent the prey and when the signal is given, they all run to hide. Each camper must be able to see the predator from his hiding spot. When all of the prey have hidden, the predator may remove his blindfold. He then scans the surrounding territory, catching his prey by naming or describing the location of anyone he can see. Anyone that is caught comes back to the center.

After a few minutes, when the predator can no longer see anyone, the predator puts his blindfold back on and the game resumes. This time, the prey that have escaped detection must change hiding places and move closer to the predator. Again, the predator removes his blindfold and scans the area calling out the name or location of anyone he can see. If some of the prey remain undetected, another round can be played. When only one of the prey remains, he is declared the winner and becomes the new predator for another game.

iStockphoto/Thinkstock

Activity #39: Animal Classifications

Cut out about 40 pictures of different animals from magazines. Ask the campers to see how many ways they can group the animals. They can try classifying the animals by what color they are, how big they are, what they have covering their bodies (e.g. feathers, hair, scales), how they move, where they live, what they eat, and which ones make good pets.

Digital Vision

Activity #40: Who Am I?

Place a sign with the name of a plant, animal, or natural object on each camper's back. Then have everyone try to figure out what their individual signs are by asking questions of others. The questions should only be yes/no questions. When nearly everyone has determined what his sign says, the signs can be switched and the game repeated.

Activity #41: Balance of Nature

This game demonstrates the concept that nature is said to be in a state of balance when the populations of animals and plants are in such proportions that everyone has food without damaging the well-being of another species. Divide the group into three equal groups, with one group representing grass, one representing mice, and one representing bobcats. Each group should have a specific physical sign that distinguishes it from the others. For example, the players in the grass group might wave their arms above their heads to look like blades of grass blowing in the wind. In designating these groups, be sure to play up the importance of the grass and the mice or everyone will want to be a bobcat.

When the game begins, the bobcats try to catch the mice, the mice try to catch the grass, and the blades of grass try to catch the bobcats. The reasoning behind the grass chasing the bobcats is that when bobcats die, their bodies fertilize the soil and provide nourishment for the grass. If a chaser succeeds in tagging his victim, the victim then changes species and becomes whatever tagged him and they both continue trying to tag more victims. It is wise to set boundaries. After a few minutes of play, call all the players back and count the number of each species that is left, and then let the tagging start again.

After a few more minutes, call them back and count them off again. Often, the previously dying species will have made a remarkable recovery. The students can see that population is important and that it establishes a balance. If only a few mice are left, plenty of grass will be available for them to eat, and their predators (the bobcats) will have a harder time finding them. Therefore, it is likely that the mice will make a comeback. This exercise can be repeated as many times as you like and different scenarios will play out each time. It can also bring about a great discussion if you introduce one predator who can tag anyone in the game. How does this addition impact the balance of nature?

Activity #42: Pond Exploration

Bodies of water represent complete ecosystems—relatively independent areas where the interrelationships of the animal and plant life and how various life forms have adapted to their environment can be studied. Using dip nets, white plastic containers, an underwater scope, and a resource book or cards describing pond life, study the creatures of the pond. Each group should capture specimens, identify them, and determine and record how they have adapted to their unique environment. The following adaptations may be reported: gills, hinged lower lip, piercing mouthparts, calcareous shell, breathing bubble, exoskeleton, hairy legs, sucking mouthparts, no head capsule, breathing tube, hairy feet, chewing mouth parts, oar-like legs, jointed legs, camouflage, air breathing, long antennae. Look for the following specimens: algae, hydras, tubifex worms, leeches, freshwater snails, daphnia, copepods, scud/amphipods, backswimmer water bugs, water boatmen, water striders, water tigers.

Ciaran Griffin

Activity #43: Underwater Scope

An underwater scope can help campers discover a whole new world of life under the water. To make one, you will need the following items: an old coffee can or other large can, plastic wrap, a rubber band, scissors, and a can opener. Use the can opener to open both ends of the can and cut a circle of plastic wrap to fit over one end of the can, making sure to leave at least an extra two inches all the way around. Stretch the plastic wrap tight like a drum and secure it with a rubber band. To make a tighter seal, tape the extra edges with duct tape. At a pond, stream, or lake, have campers stand still in a shallow area and tell them to notice the water life that they can see. Then, have them place the plastic covered end of the scope in the water, about an inch below the surface, and look down into the water through the scope. Ask the campers what they can see using the scope.

Activity #44: Tree Tag

This simple game allows the campers to test their knowledge of tree species. To play, find an open meadow bordered by trees and let the trees be the boundaries of the game. Tell them that if they touch a certain species of trees, which you will announce, that they will be "safe," but only if they are touching the right type of tree and the "right" tree will change. The counselors will serve as judges. Now, choose one person to be "it," announce which of the tree species surrounding the meadow is the "safe" species, and begin to play. You may also play this game by designating the "safe tree" by giving them information they have learned about forest ecology (e.g., a tree that provides a home for squirrels, a tree that will be the first to move into the sunny meadow, a tree that has seeds spread by birds, a tree that has an exceptionally deep root system. You can use these questions to remind the campers of any facts they have learned about the trees in your area.

Thinkstock

Activity #45: Terrarium Making

Building and maintaining a terrarium provides the opportunity to explore the differences in various soil communities and to gain an understanding of the balance and interrelationships needed to sustain even a small natural community.

Begin by exploring several different soil environments with the campers. You might look at north facing slopes, south facing slopes, the forest floor, and a meadow. Next, ask each camper which environment he wishes to recreate in his terrarium and provide a container for each person. The container can be a plastic cup, a wide-mouth glass jar, or even the bottom part of a two-liter plastic soda bottle.

Everyone should begin by putting a half an inch of gravel into the bottom of his terrarium. Then, each camper should place about two inches of soil from the environment he has chosen into his terrarium. Then, plants from that environment can be added as well as lichen, moss, small stones, etc. Make sure that campers dig carefully and get all the roots of the plants they have chosen and that they leave enough room between plants for growth.

Finally, the terrariums can be watered moderately and tightly covered with plastic wrap or some kind of lid. They should be stored in a cool, light area away from direct sunlight. The basic principles of a terrarium are conservation of moisture, protection against sudden changes in temperature, and provision for light. The plants thrive because the water that transpires from their leaves and evaporates from the soil condenses and keeps the moisture content constant.

iStockphoto/Thinkstock

Activity #46: Quartz Rush

This activity allows campers to explore the geology of the area by taking the role of prospectors. Quartz is a common mineral found in many areas, but any mineral may be used. Divide the campers into several groups (i.e., mining companies), each led by a counselor. To help create the scene, counselors may want to dress like prospectors (i.e., overalls, plaid shirts, old hats, dirt on their faces). Read the following news bulletin:

> "Nationwide Quartz Rush in Progress! Scientists working on alternative energy sources have discovered a new type of fuel that is safe, economical, inexpensive, and does not have dangerous by-products. Prospectors all over the country are searching for this precious mineral whose value has increased 100 times overnight."

The leader now shows the group a piece of quartz and explains that rich deposits of quartz are known to exist in the area, which is the break they've all been waiting for—a chance to become prospectors and strike it rich. The leader can now take the mining companies to a location where quartz (or any mineral you have chosen) can be found. Each group will choose a name for their mining company along the way.

Upon arrival at the prospecting site, discuss the difference between rocks and minerals and the different kinds of rocks (i.e., igneous, metamorphic, and sedimentary) with the campers. Then, give the campers some time to look for quartz. In most cases, quartz will not be found in its pure form but will be in combination with other minerals.

You can set up an "Assay Office" sign and have the campers bring all the quartz they find to you, the "Mad Assayer," to determine the value of their finds. You will award points on the quartz finds of individual prospectors. The prospectors, in turn, report their points to their mining company leaders and continue the search for quartz. The mad assayer can barter with the prospectors as well as help them recognize the constituent minerals of rocks in your area. After the assay office closes, the mining companies tally their points. After the assays are complete, gather the campers again and discuss their discoveries. Questions and topics of conversations can include: What is quartz? What is the difference between a rock and a mineral? What makes a mineral valuable? Why is gold valuable? Silver? Uranium? What other minerals have value? How do rocks contribute to life on Earth?

Activity #47: Soil Creature Search

More than three-quarters of the life on Earth lives in the soil, and it is important to understand the critical role soil plays in supporting all life. Mark off an area of ground that is one foot square for each camper and ask him to inspect the surface closely for any signs of life, types of rock, etc. They should each have a notebook or piece of paper to make notes about their discoveries as well as a trowel for digging.

Next, have everyone dig into the soil to a depth of one inch and record additional findings. Repeat this process at depths of two, three, four, five, and six inches. Compare the findings of the campers and determine where the soil is the richest in life.

Steve Baccon

4

Scavenger Hunts

Scavenger hunts are extremely flexible and effective teaching games. A scavenger hunt can be designed to emphasize almost any concept within the natural world and can be used in an alley or city park just as easily as in the most pristine wilderness area. The thrill of the search and the joy of discovery make them popular with both children and adults.

Although the traditional concept of a scavenger hunt has been to collect items from a list and bring them to a central place for examination and judging, many of the following scavenger hunts contain items that are *discovered* rather than *collected*. Participants may draw pictures or take digital photos of their discoveries and return these to the central location, or a group may simply discover and point them out while walking along a trail. It is important to be careful not to damage the environment while conducting a scavenger hunt.

"So many trees in sight.
So many birds in flight.
So many bugs on the ground.
So many things to be found."
—Eleven-year-old camper

Activity #48: Awareness Scavenger Hunt

- Something humans can't live without
- Something red in nature
- Evidence of an animal
- The youngest natural thing you can find
- The oldest natural thing you can find
- Something beautiful in nature
- Two seeds
- Something with a smooth texture
- Something with a rough texture
- Something that makes a sound when the wind blows
- Something that has a good smell
- Something natural that has no purpose

Andy Sotiriou

Activity #49: Sound Scavenger Hunt

- Sound made by an insect
- Sound of grass moving
- Sound of an airplane
- Sound of a motor
- Sound made by a bird
- Sound of wind blowing
- Sound made by a tree
- Sound of a stick breaking
- Sound made by a frog
- Sound made by an animal
- Sound made only by humans
- Sound of water dripping or flowing

Comstock Images

Activity #50: Rock Scavenger Hunt

- A rock that contains several different minerals
- An igneous rock
- A rock that contains pieces of a shiny mineral
- A sedimentary rock
- A rock that has been around for at least one million years
- A piece of rock that looks like it broke off another rock
- A valuable rock
- A rock that contains crystals
- Something made from rocks
- A metamorphic rock
- A rock that has eroded
- A rock with stripes

Activity #51: Web of Life Scavenger Hunt

- Something that helps a tree
- Something a rabbit might eat
- Something growing on something else
- Something that should not be where you found it
- Something humans could not live without
- Something that might be changed by the wind
- Something that provides food for a bird
- Something humans have changed
- Something that lives in a tree
- Something that has protective coloring
- An insect that helps a plant
- Something that turns sun, air, and water into food

Jupiterimages

Activity #52: Time Scavenger Hunt

- The oldest living thing around
- The youngest living thing around
- Something eroded by water
- Something that might be 100 years old
- Something that might be at least one million years old
- An example of a plant adaptation that has allowed it to thrive in the climate of the area
- Six natural items placed in order from youngest to oldest
- A sketch of what the area looked like before humans came
- Something that could have been around when dinosaurs roamed the Earth
- Something that has adapted to take advantage of the wind
- Something that has not changed over time
- A sketch of what the area will look like 100 years in the future if humans take care of it

iStockphoto/Thinkstock

Activity #53: Conservation Scavenger Hunt

- A bag of litter
- A sketch of a place where a dam has helped to stop erosion
- Something that causes erosion
- Something that prevents erosion
- Something that could cause a forest fire
- An example of soil that does not hold water well
- An example of soil that does hold water well
- A song about conservation
- A sketch of what might happen to the land if all the trees were cut down
- A piece of wood that has been infected by boring beetles
- An example of balance in nature
- A piece of grass from an area that has never been plowed
- Something that protects the soil

Mike Powell

Activity #54: Forest Scavenger Hunt

- A small piece of the "skin" of a tree
- A sign of an animal that lives in a tree
- A seed from a tree
- An estimate of the height of the tallest tree in the area
- An animal or sign of an animal that helps decompose dead trees
- A tree that is more than 100 years old
- A piece of wood that looks like an animal
- A sprig from a shade-loving tree
- A sprig from a sun-loving tree
- A made-up legend about a tree stump (to be performed)
- A part of a tree that produces food
- A sign of an animal that helps a tree

Activity #55: Nature Photography Scavenger Hunt

Take a photograph of the following things:
- A bird in a tree or on a bush
- A squirrel or another small animal
- Animal tracks
- A sunset or sunrise
- An example of interdependence in nature
- A rock that looks like a heart
- Something unusual like a tree root curled around a rock
- A cloud in the shape of an animal
- Something flying through the air
- The most beautiful place you see
- Something camouflaged to blend in with its surroundings
- A scene with at least eight different colors

Activity #56: Animal Signs Scavenger Hunt

- A set of tracks (What animal made them?)
- Scat (Did the animal eat plants or animals? Do you see seeds?)
- The remains of a squirrel or chipmunk feast
- A sign of a bird living in a tree
- A sign of an animal that lives underground
- A tree scar made by an animal
- An anthill
- A sign of an insect living in a tree
- A drawing of a wild animal seen during the hunt
- A sound made by a wild animal during the hunt (to be mimicked)
- A sign of an animal that eats plants
- An animal bone

iStockphoto/Thinkstock

Activity #57: Insect Scavenger Hunt

- An insect eating a plant
- An insect eating another insect
- An insect pollinating a flower
- An insect drinking nectar from a plant
- An insect colored to blend into its background
- An insect with two wings
- An insect with four wings
- An insect without wings
- An insect that lives in a "society"
- An example of a larval stage
- A colorful insect
- An insect that lives in trees

Activity #58: Plant Scavenger Hunt

- A seed that is specially adapted to blow in the wind
- A sketch of a plant that has lost its leaves to prevent water loss
- A leaf from a plant that has developed broad leaves to gather more sun
- A berry from a plant that has developed berries to entice animals to carry its seeds
- A leaf with serrated edges that prevents leaves from shading each other
- The height of a tall plant that gathers sunlight by rising above surrounding plants
- A sketch or a written description of a plant that has adapted to wet conditions
- A "hitchhiker seed" that travels by sticking to animals and birds
- A winged seed from a tall plant
- A leaf from a plant that has a sweet smell to attract birds and insects
- A sketch of a plant that uses color to attract insects or birds
- A plant that survives by living on another plant

Activity #59: Night Sky Scavenger Hunt

- A group of stars that looks like a dog
- Something that revolves around the Earth
- Something that revolves around the Sun
- Something in the night sky that is man-made
- The center of the galaxy
- A light in the sky that has traveled more than a year to reach the earth
- Two stars that are different colors
- Something that plays a role in the Earth's water cycle
- Something in the night sky that is at least six trillion miles away
- A body in the sky that reflects light
- A body in the sky that emits its own light
- The North Star

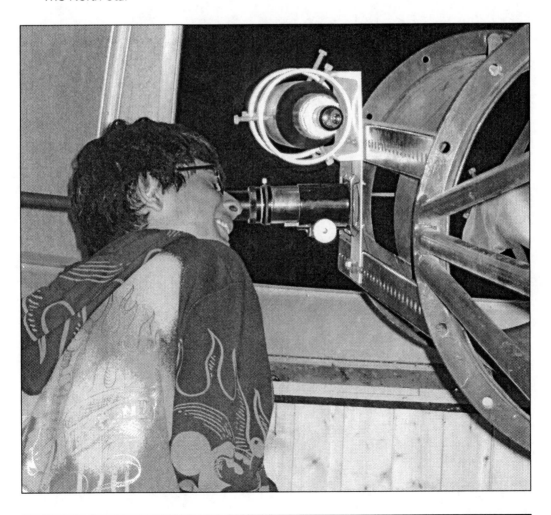

Activity #60: Beach Scavenger Hunt

- The hard protective "home" of a sea animal
- Something that is eaten by sea animals
- Rocks that have been eroded by water
- A sign of something from the sea that is eaten by humans
- Something from the sea that has flotation devices
- An animal that burrows into the sand
- A sketch of a sea bird
- An animal that lives in tide pools
- A sign of a marine mammal
- A piece of driftwood
- A piece of coral
- A stone that has been in the ocean

Activity #61: Bird Scavenger Hunt

- A feather
- Something a bird would eat
- Something that indicates a bird has been there
- A drawing or photo of a bird's home
- Something a bird might use to make its home
- The song of a bird that is heard during the hunt (to be mimicked)
- A sketch of a bird seen during the hunt
- A plant that attracts birds
- A sketch or photo of a bird that swims
- A sketch or photo of a bird that migrates
- A sketch or photo of a bird that has bright plumage to attract a mate
- A sketch or photo of the state bird

Activity #62: Meadow Scavenger Hunt

- Something in a meadow that uses color to attract insects
- The tallest piece of grass you can find
- A sign of an animal living in the meadow
- A "sticky" grass seed that travels by "hitchhiking" on animal fur
- A piece of grass with a broad leaf
- Three different colors of green
- A spiderweb
- A drawing of a butterfly seen in the meadow
- An animal home in the meadow
- A source of food for animals
- A sound tapestry of the sounds heard in the meadow
- Someone dressed up like a meadow creature

Activity #63: Winter Scavenger Hunt

- Animal tracks in the snow
- An icicle
- Brown leaves still hanging from a tree
- A "leaf" that stays green all winter
- Seven different colors in the winter landscape
- Three tree buds waiting for spring
- A tunnel or hole in the snow (What do you think made it?)
- A sign of insects
- A hole in a tree where an animal might shelter from bad weather
- A sign of spring
- Something natural that is red
- A photo or sketch of a snowman you make

Creatas Images

Activity #64: Really Big All-Inclusive Nature Scavenger Hunt

- A piece of wood that looks like an animal
- An insect, animal, or bird that is camouflaged in its surroundings
- A natural object that has five parts
- An object that has at least four visible colors
- A natural sound that makes you feel happy
- Three different leaves
- Three different seeds
- An animal bone
- Someone dressed up like a tree
- A color drawing of a wildflower
- A wild berry
- Ten pieces of litter
- A rock that contains crystals
- An insect home
- A leaf from a plant that lives near water
- The height of the tallest tree you can see
- Something you find in nature that should not be there
- Something pink in nature
- Something in nature that provides food for another living creature
- A work of art inspired by nature (drawn/painted by one of your group)
- A "scar" on a tree made by an animal
- Three different kinds of rocks
- A song about nature (written and performed by the group)
- A poem about a tree (written and performed by the group)

5

Along the Trail

Hiking is one of the most basic forms of outdoor recreation. It promotes a healthy lifestyle and offers the best way to get up close and personal with nature. Often when hiking, people tend to focus on the destination—the top of a mountain or a waterfall at the end of a trail. Yet, so many teachable moments occur naturally during the hike and may be taken advantage of along the way. The activities in this section encourage campers to slow down and appreciate everything around them. Whether embarking on a 20-minute themed hike, a daylong excursion, or a five-day backpacking trip, these activities will enhance the journey.

"I am in love with this world … I have nestled lovingly in it. …
I have climbed its mountains, roamed its forests, sailed
its waters, crossed its deserts, felt the sting of its frosts,
the oppression of its heats, the drench of its rains,
the fury of its winds, and always have beauty
and joy waited upon my goings and comings."
—John Burroughs

Activity #65: Smell Hike

Take the campers on a hike that makes them focus on their sense of smell in order to find their way along a trail. What does the bark of a tree smell like? (A ponderosa pine is said to smell like vanilla or butterscotch.) What does sage smell like? What do flowers and grasses smell like? Why do different plants have different smells? Are they trying to attract insects?

Jupiterimages

Activity #66: Follow Your Nose

Divide the group in half. Using an onion or another object with a strong smell, have one group rub the onion on trees to mark the trail. The other group must follow the trail by sniffing out the scent. Then, have the groups switch roles.

Activity #67: Nature Bingo

Many common games can be adapted for use in the outdoors, and bingo is a great example. The campers can either use bingo cards that you have made ahead of time or they can create cards themselves. If they are making their own cards, provide a list of items that you would like them to find or things they think they might find. Then, they can draw or write the items on their bingo cards. See how many bingos they can get throughout the hike.

B	I	N	G	O
a Ladybug	a rock that looks like a heart	an acorn	Tracks	a Spider's web
an edible plant _____		ants	a bird's nest	Sage
a feather	a clover	Free	a robin	a piece of granite
State Flower	Scat	a rose bush	a mushroom	Douglas Fir Pine cone
yellow flower		a bird singing	remains of a squirrel feast	Seeds on a plant

Activity #68: The Stick Game

While hiking, have each camper pick up a stick that he thinks resembles an object. He must then use his stick as though it were that object. For example, a camper may find a stick that looks like a big spoon, so he would pretend like he was eating from it, or a camper may find a stick that looks like a broom, so he would pretend like he was sweeping with it. Campers can either explain what their sticks are supposed to be or have others guess.

iStockphoto/Thinkstock

Activity #69: Memory Hike

When out hiking in the wilderness, whether it is in the mountains, in the forest, or in the desert, it is important to pay attention to where you are going and where you have been. For this hike, tell the campers that they will be hiking for a certain distance and when they get to that point, they will be asked questions about certain objects along the trail to test their observation skills. As a variation, have each camper think of 10 questions of his own after the hike. Have the campers write down their questions, and then exchange with each other. Following are some sample questions:

- What color were the flowers in the middle of the trail?
- On which side of the trail was the tree with the bird's nest in it?
- How many different types of trees did you count?
- Was there scat on the trail? If so, from what animal?

Activity #70: Insect Hike

Explain to campers that they are constantly surrounded by insects, whether sitting still, hiking along a forest trail, or walking across sand dunes by the ocean. Have campers take a closer look at the insects they find and sketch them while observing them. What are the purposes of their different body parts? What color are the insects and why?

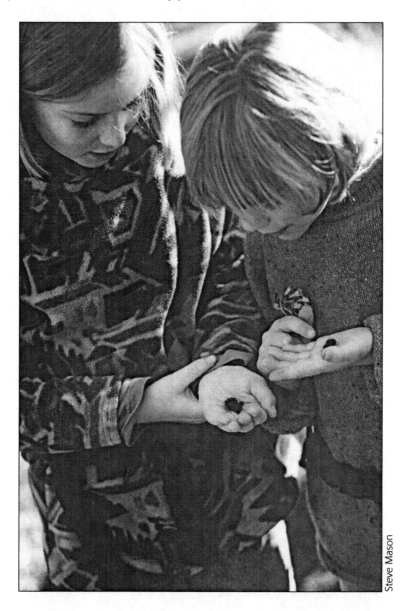

Steve Mason

Activity #71: Alphabet Hike

Before heading out on a hike, hand each camper a piece of paper with each letter of the alphabet listed and explain to them that they are to find at least one item in nature for every letter. The real name of the item must be used (e.g., cat, not kitty). Depending on the age of the campers, you can make it more challenging by saying it has to be specific like red-tailed hawk, not just hawk. After the hike, debrief what they found. What letter was the hardest? Which letter do they have the most items for? What item was their most exciting find?

Activity #72: FBI Hike

This fun activity can take place anywhere. The FBI (Forest Bureau of Investigation) can also become the CIA (City Investigation Agency). Campers are challenged to explore their environment to find evidence of "criminal activity" within the natural world. Examples might include trees that are *littering* by carelessly scattering needles or leaves, birds that are *murdering* insects or worms, or squirrels that are *kidnapping* children (i.e., the seeds of trees). The possibilities are endless and can lead to discussions about food chains, interrelationships within the natural world, and many other natural principles. Investigators can use digital cameras to document the crime scene and make notes about the evidence they find. At the end of the hike, the detectives make wanted posters describing each criminal they uncovered.

WANTED

Information Leading to the Arrest and Conviction of:

Name: Molothrus Ater Artemisia

Alias: Brown Headed Cowbird

Identifying Marks:
Length 6 to 8 inches.
Male: irridescent black, purple and green.
Female: dark brown-grey, lighter below.

Crime:
Child Abandonment

Last Reported:
Near corrals and livestock. Often returns to the same area year after year. Usually in flocks or gangs of 15 or more.

Modus Operandi:
Sneaks in and lays eggs in the nests of other birds.

Activity #73: Orchestral Outing

To begin, have the campers sit and listen to the sounds around them. Whether you are in a park in the middle of a city or a meadow surrounded by trees, ask the campers to listen for sounds that inspire their inner musician. While hiking, have the campers collect items from nature that they can use to make noise (e.g., by tapping the items together, by blowing through them, or by using other creative means). At the end of the hike, allot time for the campers to create a piece of music using everything they found and perform it.

Activity #74: Tracking

Nothing enlivens the senses like the anticipation of surprises, and tracking games provide this type of excitement. One of the most interesting kinds of tracking is, of course, the following of animal trails. Unfortunately, this activity is not possible in all areas. However, tracking games played by two individuals or teams are practical in almost any location. One popular tracking game involves two teams. The first team gets a 10- or 15-minute head start to lay their trail. They may set up prearranged indications of their path, such as rocks arranged in a definite pattern, or they may try to proceed as secretly as possible, leaving only inadvertent evidence of their passage. Some types of terrain are very good for this secretive movement. In other types of terrain, however, it is virtually impossible for the tracking team to follow unless markers have been laid. At the end of their trail, the first team hides and awaits the approach of the tracking team. The tracking team follows the trail left by the first team as closely as possible, and the game ends when they successfully find the hiding team. Teams may reverse roles for a second go-around.

iStockphoto/Thinkstock

Activity #75: Plant Tag

Lay out a course about a quarter of a mile long. Starting at "home base," players go on a nature walk along the course, during which 10 to 15 flowers, trees, and other plants are pointed out and named. At the far end of the course, one player is designated as "it." The object of the game is to get back to home base without being tagged by "it." Players are safe whenever they are touching one of the identified plants. The person who is "it" may challenge players to name the plant they are touching. If they fail to do so, they are considered tagged. Anyone who gets tagged becomes "its" helper and may tag other players.

iStockphoto/Thinkstock

Activity #76: Biomimicry Hike

Biomimicry is the science and art of emulating nature's best biological ideas, systems, models, processes, and elements to solve human problems, create more efficient ways of completing everyday tasks, and come up with new inventions. For example, a tree is an example of a living water pump, and Olympic swimming suits were designed after studying sharks. Before setting out on the hike, tell campers that at the end of the hike they will be asked to come up with their own invention or innovation inspired by the natural world. As you hike along, have campers look for items in nature that inspire ideas that humans can use. Encourage the group to be creative and to share their ideas. At the end of the hike, campers can draw or write about their nature-inspired inventions.

Photodisc

Activity #77: Un-Nature Hike

Before heading out on this hike, the leader should place man-made items along the trail. These items can be hidden partially under rocks, in trees, or in bushes. Explain to the campers that as they walk, they should be looking for these items and writing down what they find and where they find it. Campers should be spaced out and quiet as they hike. This activity can be used to talk about environmental concepts or for conversations about camouflage if the items are similar in shape and color to the natural things they are hidden in.

iStockphoto/Thinkstock

6

Nature at Night

Seldom do children have the opportunity to experience the wonders of the nocturnal world. Many children are unfamiliar and uncomfortable with being outdoors once the sun has set. Yet, nocturnal animals, starry skies, and the events that take place between dusk and dawn are fascinating aspects of nature. It is not only fun to discover animals at night, but it is also fun to notice human reactions. It is interesting to learn what the body does to compensate for darkness and how the senses are heightened. Nighttime nature discovery will spark imagination in new ways and unfold the mysteries of nature at night. It is important to make sure campers feel safe and secure and that the group feels at ease. Taking time to introduce campers to the night environment will help to expand the campers' comfort zones and help shift fear to wonder.

"My companion and I were alone with the stars: the misty river of the Milky Way flowing across the sky, the patterns of the constellations standing out bright and clear, a blazing planet low on the horizon. It occurred to me that if this were a sight that could be seen only once in a century, that this little headland would be thronged with spectators. But it can be seen many scores of nights in any year, and so the lights burned in the cottages and the inhabitants probably gave not a thought to the beauty overhead; and because they can see it almost any night, perhaps they never will."
—Rachel Carson

Activity #78: Night Vision

Have campers sit in a circle and cover one eye with one hand and keep it covered while having a discussion of eye function (e.g., rods, cones, pupil dilation, etc.). After the discussion, keeping the one eye covered, light a candle in the center of the circle and have ca pers look at it for about three minutes with their uncovered eye. Blow the candle out and have the campers look around, alternating opening and closing each eye. Campers will see and feel the difference between night vision and day vision simultaneously.

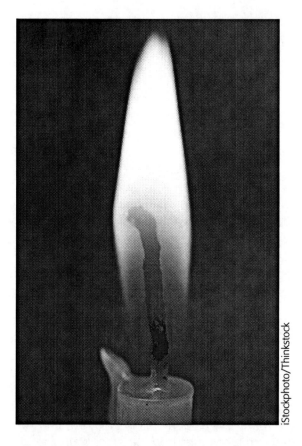

iStockphoto/Thinkstock

Activity #79: Colored Paper Guess

In a dark space, either outdoors with only the light from the moon and stars or indoors in an almost completely dark room, hand each camper a piece of colored paper and ask him to guess what color he thinks it is. Then, have the campers put the piece of paper into their pockets. At the end of the evening's activities, when campers have returned to an indoor setting or when the lights have been turned on, have them check their pieces of paper and see if they were right about the color.

Activity #80: Bat and Moth Game

This activity works best if the leader first explains *echolocation*. Echolocation is the process some animals use to judge the location of objects, as well as to determine an object's identity, the distance between the animal and the object, and the direction an object is moving. For example, bats emit sound waves through either their nose or mouth and then wait for the echo to return to them.

Have a camper volunteer to be a bat. The bat is then blindfolded and placed in the center of the circle. Next, have someone volunteer to be a moth. Both the bat and the moth are given a film canister or paper cup filled with gravel to use as a communication device. When the bat shakes his canister or cup, the moth must answer by shaking his canister or cup. They continue this process, moving around the circle until the bat catches the moth by tagging him.

iStockphoto/Thinkstock

Activity #81: Deer Ears

Many animals rely on the cover of night for protection from predators or to find their prey. However, thriving at night requires a highly developed sense of hearing. Animals such as deer and bats have much larger ears to compensate for their lack of vision at night.

First, have campers close their eyes and listen. How many sounds can they hear? Next, have campers cup their hands behind their ears, much like what a deer's ears would look like. Now how many sounds can they hear? Which method gives them better hearing? Not only do deer have larger ears, but also they are able to move them in different directions to pick up more sounds.

iStockphoto/Thinkstock

Activity #82: Disappearing Heads

Have the campers stand in two rows facing each other about eight feet apart. Instruct them to stand completely still and stare at the face of the person across from them. Their partner's head should slowly disappear. Explain why this happens: Rods in the eyes see light and cones see color. When you are staring straight ahead, you use the cones and ignore the rods. At night however, light is more important than color. In a sense, your eyes are turning off the light, making the object seem to disappear.

Activity #83: Smell Test

Before heading out for a night hike, fill up film canisters or similar containers with various scented items (e.g., spices from the kitchen or items found in nature such as sage). Have the campers form a circle, and then pass the canisters around one at a time and have the campers smell them. No one should talk while a canister is going around the circle. When a canister makes it all the way around the circle, let the campers guess what was in it and then repeat for each canister.

Activity #84: Hidden Owl

During the hike, have the campers divide into two groups. They should remain with their groups throughout the activity. One group hides first and, once hidden, they must call attention to themselves every 60 seconds by hooting like an owl. The other group tries to find them by focusing on listening for them. Once the group has been found, they switch places and the other group hides.

Comstock Images

Activity #85: Star Charades

In this variation of charades, one player pantomimes the name of a common constellation, star, or planet. Other players try to guess what the charade is. Possibilities include: the Big Dipper, the Little Dipper, Leo the lion, Draco the dragon, Taurus the bull, Orion the hunter, Gemini the twins, Pisces the fish, Aries the ram, the Milky Way, Jupiter, Mars, and many more.

Activity #86: Star Stories

Many legends about the stars exist and make terrific stories around a campfire. After telling a few Greek or Indian legends, your group can have a lot of fun making up legends. They can be new stories about real constellations like the Great Bear, the Lion, the Eagle, etc., or the group can find its own constellation (e.g., Alfred the aardvark or Theodore the toad) and make up a legend to explain its presence in the night sky.

One good way to get everyone involved in the storytelling is to begin the story and then stop in a critical place, usually mid-sentence. The person to the right of the original storyteller then picks up the story, adds to it, and again stops in a critical place and passes the story to the next person. In this way, the story progresses around the entire campfire circle until the last person finishes it.

Hemera/Thinkstock

Activity #87: Oatmeal Box Planetariums

Creating a planetarium out of an oatmeal box is a great way to start learning about and identifying constellations found in the night sky.

- Cut a hole in the bottom of an empty round oatmeal box. The 42-ounce containers are the best size for this activity. The hole should be the size of the light source you are going to use (i.e., small if using a pen light or larger if using a flashlight).
- Remove the paper from the lid, leaving the plastic ring with a big circle cut out of it (Figure A).

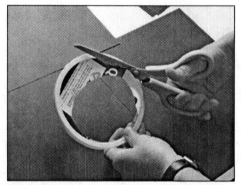

Figure A

- Next, using the lid as a guide, trace a circle on dark-colored cardstock (Figure B) and cut it out. The cardstock circle will be the constellation card, so cut out as many as needed.

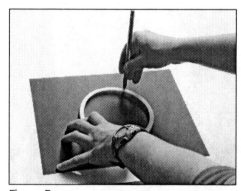

Figure B

- Now, using a sharp pointed object (e.g., needle, pin, end of a paper clip) and with a star chart as a guide, punch holes into the constellation card (Figure C). If a star is more prominent, it can be a larger hole and fainter stars should have smaller holes.

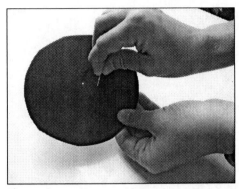

Figure C

- Place the constellation card on the underside of the lid and then place the lid on the oatmeal container (Figure D).

Figure D

- In a dark room, shine the light through the bottom of the oatmeal box while pointing the constellation end toward a blank wall or ceiling, which will project the constellation onto the surface.

This activity is a great bedtime activity for counselors to use with campers. They can project the constellations onto the tent or cabin ceiling and ask if anyone can name them. After learning the constellations, be sure to take the campers out at night to find the constellations in the sky.

7

Nature and Art

Artists have been inspired by nature for centuries. Nature itself is a work of art offering vibrant colors, intricate shapes, unique lighting, and interesting textures. Using natural objects to create pieces of art or crafts provides opportunities for campers to express themselves in various mediums. When given motivation to observe and interpret designs from nature, children who do not normally excel in the arts have a tendency to be more creative than when creating art in a classroom setting. Creating art *from* nature and *in* nature provides many important lessons including developing an eye for composition as well as attention to detail.

Throughout the previous chapters, the activities have talked about senses, perspective, and connections related to the natural world. Art in nature encompasses all of these elements, allowing a unique opportunity for creativity through multisensory experiences resulting in a concrete expression of a camper's interpretation of the world around him.

> *"As I sit in my special spot, I see the world from new points of view. I see how much detail there really is in nature. I see the beauty of life in a new, special way. How the sun fills up the meadows and how the snow glitters as clouds drift by. I have never experienced such beauty and wonder before."*
> —Sixth grade student

Activity #88: Nature Rubbings

Creating nature rubbings is a simple way for children to explore texture and patterns in nature. First, go on a hike to collect items such as rocks, leaves, bark, sticks, and shells. Then, give each camper a sheet of paper to place over one of the items. Have them rub evenly over the paper with chalk, pastels, charcoal, colored pencils, or paint. Encourage them to have fun experimenting with different mediums. They can make single rubbings, try to layer their rubbings to create a collage, or make a picture using the items to form a scene. They can also cut out single rubbings and glue them onto paper to make stationery.

Activity #89: Sumi-e Painting

This activity gives campers the opportunity to capture the essence of wildlife using simple brush strokes. Sumi-e is an ancient classic art and, though it can take a lifetime to master, beginners can achieve impressive results. The enjoyment of this type of art is in capturing the essential nature of the subject immediately and simply.

With a brief lesson on how to load the big, soft brush with water and ink (or acrylic), students can swirl and twist delightful forms on newsprint, where the empty space becomes as important as the subject. A touch of wet ink on porous paper will form a small, furry body; another touch becomes a head; then whiskers, feet, tail, and eyes are whisked on with a load of black ink on the brush tip.

The movements are rapid and free with great possibilities for individual results. Books on Sumi-e are available and the equipment is simple: a stone (or dish), a brick of ink (or tubes of acrylics), a Sumi-e brush, and newsprint.

Hemera/Thinkstock

Activity #90: Nature Mobiles

Kids love to collect items from hikes that mean something to them, and this activity is a simple way to display pressed flowers, leaves, pinecones, seashells, small rocks, and other prized possessions, which also makes it a great activity to pair with a scavenger hunt.

After a nature scavenger hunt, have campers create a mobile. First, have campers find a stick that is of interest to them and large enough to hang their objects from. Using thread or fishing line, have them tie the objects to the stick. This activity also reinforces concepts such as gravity, symmetry, balance, fulcrum points, and motion.

Activity #91: Sun Printing

For this activity, you will need the following materials:

- Sunprint® Kit (www.sunprints.org) or light-sensitive paper (such as NaturePrint® Paper, www.natureprintpaper.com) and a piece of plexiglass or plastic wrap
- Flat pan or tub
- Sun or light
- Cardboard

The light-sensitive paper goes through a chemical change when exposed to light, so campers should make sure not to expose the paper until the picture that they want to capture has been laid out on it. Prints can be made outdoors on a sunny or overcast day or indoors on a sunny windowsill. The prints can be framed or used to make stationery.

Give campers the following instructions:
- Select an item or items that you wish to use. Leaves and ferns are interesting because of the shapes and details that come through.
- Place a piece of cardboard down first.
- Place the light-sensitive paper with the blue side up.
- Lay the items on the paper in the desired pattern and top with the plexiglass.
- Expose the paper until it turns almost white (about five minutes indoors and up to 20 minutes outdoors on a cloudy day). Be careful not to overexpose the paper.
- Quickly rinse the paper in the water pan for about one minute and lay flat to dry.

Activity #92: Rustic Stick Frames

Help the campers gather sticks about ¼ to 1¼ inches thick and break them into equal lengths. Have each camper form his sticks in the shape of a picture frame. If he is using thinner sticks, he might want to put more than one on each side; whereas with thicker sticks, he might choose to use just one per side. When the sticks are in place, tack them together with a glue gun. Campers can then wrap the four corners with twine/sinew and cut and glue a six-inch piece of twine to the back of the frame for hanging.

Activity #93: Journal Making

For this activity, you will need the following materials:
- A piece of 8½ x 11 inch cardstock for the cover
- White paper for inside the journal
- Contact paper or Mod Podge®
- A thin, sturdy stick about an inch longer than the binding edge of the paper
- Hemp or other natural looking twine
- Dried leaves, grass, pressed flowers, or other flat items found in nature

Journal One: Contact Paper

First, have the campers lay out the natural items on the cardstock in whatever pattern or arrangement they desire. Next, cut a piece of the contact paper about a half an inch wider on each side than the sheet of paper. Help each camper place the contact paper on top of the decorated cover and, starting from the bottom, slide his fingers up the paper to press out any air bubbles. He then folds the cover in half, as well as the pages for the inside, and puts them together.

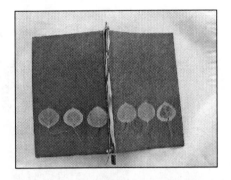

Next, help each camper tie one end of the twine up against the crease of the cover so that the twine is flush with the top of the cover. He should feed the twine inside the journal down the crease of the center page and attach it to the other end of the stick, keeping it tight enough so that the whole book is bound to the stick in a manner that holds the pages with little movement. Next, have the campers decorate the inside of the pages with leaves or flowers by

placing the items on a page and covering them with contact paper. It also adds a nice touch for campers to write nature quotes on pages throughout the journal.

Journal Two: Mod Podge

To make this variation, follow the same instructions as in Journal One for decorating, but instead of using contact paper, paint over the leaves and decorations on the front and back of the cover with Mod Podge. Another option is to fold the cover in half and, using a hole punch, place holes down the creased edge and tie with twine or ribbon to hold the journal together.

Activity #94: Nature Sculptures

Begin this activity by discussing what environmental art is with the campers. Explain that different styles of this art form exist and it can be traced back to the late 1960s. Environmental art is often used to raise awareness of topics such as the sacredness of nature, recycling, climate change, renewable energy, the importance of connecting with nature, and other important issues. Artists such as Andy Goldsworthy, Chris Drury, and Richard Long have written books that you can take on your hike to show the campers examples of art in nature.

Hike along a trail, stopping to observe natural materials, looking for unusual colors, patterns, textures, and shapes. Then, either as pairs or individuals, plan a sculpture that will not damage the environment around you. Questions to ask the campers might include: How does your sculpture represent your relationship with the environment? What do you hope your work will say to others?

Activity #95: Plaster Casts of Animal Tracks

Take the campers on an animal track hike. Once a nice, clear animal track has been found, mix plaster of Paris according to the package directions. It should be about the consistency of pancake batter. Place a can that has been opened on both ends gently around the track and into the soil or sand just a bit, which will help keep the plaster contained. Then, fill the track with about an inch of plaster. Let it dry for 30 minutes or until the plaster has hardened. Gently lift the cast out of the track and brush it off to clean it. Ask them: How many toes does the track have? Can you see claws? How big is the track? Can you guess what animal made the track? Can you tell what the animal was doing when it made the track?

iStockphoto/Thinkstock

Activity #96: Nature Puppets

Creating a puppet show from "found objects" stretches the imagination in many ways. Each camper begins by picking up a stick or a rock that can become a base for his puppet. Campers should continue to find rocks, sticks, pine needles, leaves, or anything else they will need to make their puppets come to life. Using a hot glue gun or glue, attach the items to the stick or rock. Allow each camper to devise a story around the theme of the lesson or activity and present his puppet show to the others.

Activity #97: Rock Necklaces

Have the campers choose a rock that they think will look good as a charm on a necklace. The only other materials needed for this activity are a spool of 22 to 26 gauge wire, a small pair of needle-nose pliers, pencils, and ribbon or hemp to string the finished rock.

Necklace #1

To create the necklace shown on the left side of Figure A, give campers the following instructions:

Figure A

- Cut the wire into approximately 24-inch pieces.
- Fold the wire in half and then in half again.
- Take the end with two loops and place it over the index finger, and then twist the wire together all the way down.
- Place the rock at the midpoint of the wire, and using the needle-nose pliers or your fingers, wrap the wire around the midsection of the rock, finding little notches in the rock to help hold the wire tight. Tightly twist together the two ends like a twist tie, leaving a single strand of wire at the top of the rock.
- Fold the single strand over a pencil to form a loop.
- Wind the remaining wire tightly around itself at the base.
- Remove the pencil and run the ribbon or hemp through to tie it on.

Necklace #2

To create the necklace shown on the right side of Figure A, give campers the following instructions:

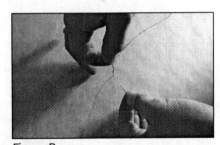

Figure B

- Cut two pieces of wire approximately 15 inches long.
- Find the midpoint of each piece and twist them together. It should now look like four wires coming out from the middle (Figure B).
- Place the rock where the wires are twisted and hold the rock in place on the bottom using your index finger (Figure C).

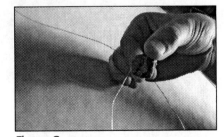

Figure C

- Holding the rock and wire with the twist horizontal, take one strand from each side and twist together. Repeat with the other two strands, beginning to form a basket around the rock. Continue to twist one strand from the previous twist until the basket reaches the top (Figures D and E).
- Pull all four strands together and twist into one strand about three inches long (Figure F).
- Fold the strand over to create a bunny ear-type loop and wrap the remaining wire tightly around the base of the loop several times (Figures G and H).
- Using wire cutters, trim off any excess wire and pinch the end down (Figure I).
- Thread ribbon or hemp through the loop.

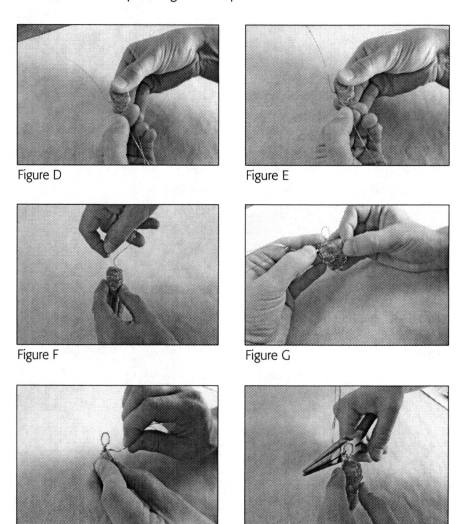

Figure D

Figure E

Figure F

Figure G

Figure H

Figure I

Activity #98: Paper Making

Paper is made by chopping up wood into chips and then mashing them together with water to make a mushy substance called *pulp*. The pulp is usually mixed with chemicals and cooked before it is put into a papermaking machine. To recycle paper, a similar process can be followed by mixing mashed-up paper with water instead of wood chips. Not only is this activity a fun craft project, but also it is a great lesson in environmental stewardship, and it helps the campers to gain a better appreciation of the resources it takes to make paper.

Give campers the following instructions:

- Make a screen using a picture frame. Use whatever size picture frame that you want the paper to be (e.g., 8 x 10, 5 x 7, 4 x 6). Remove the glass from the frame and stretch window screen tightly across it and tack it in place with a stapler.
- Rip up pieces of paper (e.g., newspaper, recycled printing paper, tissue paper, egg cartons) and allow them to soak in water for at least an hour.
- Place the ripped paper in a blender with a small amount of water. More water can be added if needed, but the pulp needs to be thick enough to adhere to the screen.
- When the mixture is thoroughly blended and liquefied, pour the pulp into a flat pan or plastic container that will allow for complete submersion of the screen.
- Pull the screen through the liquid, allowing a thin layer of the pulp to settle onto the stretched screen.
- After the screen has been removed from the water/pulp mixture, flowers, leaves, or grass can be added before drying to add interest.
- Allow the paper to dry for several hours before removing it from the screen.

iStockphoto/Thinkstock

Activity #99: Nature Kaleidoscopes

For this activity, you will need the following materials:
- Clear contact paper
- Metallic contact paper
- Duct tape or masking tape
- Scissors
- Straight pins
- Two 4 x 6 index cards

In addition, each camper should gather flowers, petals, pine needles, leaves, and grasses to place in his kaleidoscope.

Give campers the following instructions:
- Cut two 4 x 6 index cards in half lengthwise and discard one of the pieces so that only three remain.
- Cut three pieces of metallic contact paper the same size (2 x 6 inches) and stick one strip to each of the three index cards (Figure A).
- Lay all three pieces with the shiny side down without any space in between them.
- Cut three pieces of duct tape or masking tape six inches long.
- Using one piece of tape, tape two of the index card pieces together.
- Tape each side of the index cards tightly until they are in the shape of a triangle with the shiny sides in (Figure B).
- Cut out two circles from the clear contact paper 4½ to 5 inches in diameter. (Tracing a CD works well.)
- Peel off the back paper from one of the circles and place it sticky side up. Cut a half-inch (or smaller) piece of cardstock in the shape of a triangle or diamond and place it in the center to give it stability.

Figure A

Figure B

- Place flowers, petals, leaves, and grass randomly or in an arranged pattern on the circle. Make sure not to leave too much empty space (Figure C).
- When the contact paper is completely covered, place the other circle of the contact paper on top of the petals to seal it. Start from one side and gently apply pressure to eliminate any air pockets (Figure D).
- Put the straight pin through the center of the half-inch triangle and connect it in one of the corners of the triangle. Weave the pin in and out of the tape to connect it so the circle can spin freely (Figure E).

Figure C

Figure D

Figure E

Activity #100: Nature Hangings

Cover a hard surface with newspapers or paper bags and then place a piece of muslin flat on top them. Campers can lay petals, whole flowers, and leaves in whatever patterns they would like. Next, fold the material in half to cover the flowers, and using a hammer, bang the flowers and leaves so that pigment is transferred to the material. Open the material to expose two prints of the design. The finished piece can be turned into a pillow or, by folding over the top and stitching a sleeve for a stick, it can become a wall hanging.

Activity #101: Ice Garden

To begin, help campers fill containers of varying sizes and shapes with one to two inches of water, and place these containers outdoors overnight. In the morning, carefully remove the frozen disks by running warm water over the bottoms of the containers until the disks come out easily. Have the group arrange the disks outdoors as if they were setting up a garden.

Set out new containers of water each night to add to the ice garden each day. The disks will crack and take new shapes as the sun hits them, creating a display that changes every day.

About the Authors

Jane Sanborn is the executive director of the Colorado Outdoor Education Center (COEC)—a nonprofit corporation that operates three major programs: Sanborn Western Camps, High Trails Outdoor Education Center, and The Nature Place Conference Center. During her 40-year career with COEC, she spent many years as director and program director of Sanborn Western Camps. She serves on the ACA Children and Nature Task Force and has written two other books: *Bag of Tricks* and *Bag of Tricks II*.

Elizabeth Rundle has worked in the camping industry since 2002 and is currently the director of the junior program at Sanborn Western Camps. She is also an instructor with the High Trails Outdoor Education Center, an experiential-based school program. Elizabeth has presented at several national and regional ACA conferences. Her goal is to help campers and staff members take the time to slow down and make relevant and meaningful connections with the natural world.